The Legend of the Donkey's Cross

An Easter Story

The Legend of the Donkey's Cross

Judy Buck-Glenn

𝄞 Abingdon Press
Nashville

The Legend of the Donkey's Cross

Copyright © 1996 by Cokesbury

ISBN 0-687-08347-8

Book design by Paige Easter

99 00 01 02 03 04 05 06 07 08 - 10 9 8 7 6 5 4 3 2 1

Manufactured in Hong Kong

The Bible Story
Mark 11:1-10, 15-19

When they were approaching Jerusalem, at Bethphage and Bethany, near the Mount of Olives, he sent two of his disciples and said to them, "Go into the village ahead of you, and immediately as you enter it, you will find tied there a colt that has never been ridden; untie it and bring it. If anyone says to you, 'Why are you doing this?' just say this, 'The Lord needs it and will send it back here immediately.'" They went away and found a colt tied near a door, outside in the street. As they were untying it, some of the bystanders said to them, "What are you doing, untying the colt?" They told them what Jesus had said; and they allowed them to take it. Then they brought the colt to

Jesus and threw their cloaks on it; and he sat on it. Many people spread their cloaks on the road, and others spread leafy branches that they had cut in the fields. Then those who went ahead and those who followed were shouting,

"Hosanna!
Blessed is the one who comes
in the name of the Lord!
Blessed is the coming kingdom
of our ancestor David!
Hosanna in the highest
heaven!"

Verses 1–10

Then they came to Jerusalem. And he entered the temple and began to drive out those who were selling and those who were buying in the temple, and he over-turned the tables of the moneychangers and the seats of those who sold doves; and he would not allow anyone to carry anything through the temple. He was teaching and saying, "Is it not written,

'My house shall be called a
    house of prayer for all the
    nations'?
But you have made it a den of
    robbers.''

And when the chief priests and the scribes heard it, they kept looking for a way to kill him; for they were afraid of him, because the whole crowd was spellbound by his teaching. And when evening came, Jesus and his disciples went out of the city.

Verses 15-19

The Donkey's Cross

"Her name is Sarah. Come and pet her," Mr. Jefferson said, but Rachel was afraid. Some people made fun of her, but Mr. Jefferson seemed to understand. "Climb up on the fence," he urged.

Rachel climbed up. The donkey was looking right at her.

"She has pretty eyes," Rachel said. "Soft and brown. They look sad."

"Yes they do," said Mr. Jefferson. "And look at her back. See how the darker color looks like a cross. Do you know the legend of the cross on the donkey's back?"

"What's a legend?" Rachel asked.

"It is a story that has been told for a long time. The story may not be true, but it teaches us something or helps us remember something," Mr. Jefferson answered.

"When we talk about the legend of the donkey's cross, the first thing we want to think about is the Bible story that it helps us remember.

"When Jesus was coming to Jerusalem, he sent two disciples to a village to find a young donkey. If anyone asked questions, they were to say, 'The Lord needs to borrow it.'

"They brought the donkey, and Jesus rode her into Jerusalem. Jesus was a king, but not like other kings, who rode in chariots and led armies. Most of the people waved palms to greet him and called out,

'Hosanna!

Blessed is the one who comes in the name of the Lord.'

"But some of the powerful leaders were afraid that the people would follow Jesus, not them."

Rachel hardly noticed that Mr. Jefferson was bringing the donkey Sarah closer. Mr. Jefferson went on with the story.

"When Jesus got to Jerusalem, he went to the Temple. He saw people changing money and buying and selling animals. Jesus turned over all their tables, and the money scattered everywhere. He made the people who were selling things leave. 'God's house is not a market!' he said. 'God's house is a place for prayer!' Some people cheered, but others were angry. They decided to kill Jesus.

"What Jesus did took a lot of courage."

"Here, Rachel, pet Sarah's nose. She likes that."

And before she knew quite how it happened, Rachel was stroking Sarah's velvety nose.

Mr. Jefferson said, "The legend of the donkey's cross says that before Jesus died donkeys were plain gray. Ever since, donkeys have had a cross on their backs. The legend isn't part of the Bible story, it is just a story, but when we see the cross on the donkey's back, it reminds us of Jesus' courage and his love for us all."

Gently, Rachel stroked Sarah's back. Then she said the bravest thing she had ever said: "Do you think Sarah would let me ride her?"

Mr. Jefferson smiled. A minute later, Rachel was sitting on Sarah's back. And Rachel wasn't afraid at all.

A Note to Adults

Read this story with your children and then talk about what they have learned. Help them to recognize that Jesus' love for and trust in God made Jesus strong and confident. Help them to recognize that Mr. Jefferson's loving, understanding ways taught Rachel to be more trusting and confident. Here are some questions you might want to use as conversation starters.

"Why didn't Jesus just walk into the city like everyone else?"

"Do you think Jesus knew some people would be angry?"

"Why did Jesus turn over the tables in the temple?"

"Did it take courage to do what Jesus did?"

"Why do you think he was able to do it?"

"Did it take courage for Rachel to ride the donkey?"

"Why was she able to do it?"

"Did you ever have to do something that took courage?"

"What helped you to do that?"